OEDIPUS REX

SOPHOCLES

D1713828

Translated by
FRANCIS STORR

OEDIPUS REX

ARGUMENT

To Laius, King of Thebes, an oracle foretold that the child born to him by his queen Jocasta would slay his father and wed his mother. So when in time a son was born the infant's feet were riveted together and he was left to die on Mount Cithaeron. But a shepherd found the babe and tended him, and delivered him to another shepherd who took him to his master, the King of Corinth. Polybus being childless adopted the boy, who grew up believing that he was indeed the King's son. Afterwards doubting his parentage he inquired of the Delphic god and heard himself the word declared before to Laius. Wherefore he fled from what he deemed his father's house and in his flight he encountered and unwillingly slew his father Laius. Arriving at Thebes he answered the riddle of the Sphinx and the grateful Thebans made their deliverer king. So he reigned in the room of Laius, and espoused the widowed queen. Children were born to them and Thebes prospered under his rule, but again a grievous plague fell upon the city. Again the oracle was consulted and it bade them purge themselves of blood-guiltiness. Oedipus denounces the crime of which he is unaware, and undertakes to track out the criminal. Step by step it is brought home to him that he is the man. The closing scene reveals Jocasta slain by her own hand and Oedipus blinded by his own act and praying for death or exile.

DRAMATIS PERSONAE

Oedipus.
The Priest of Zeus.
Creon.
Chorus of Theban Elders.
Teiresias.
Jocasta.
Messenger.
Herd of Laius.
Second Messenger.

Scene: Thebes. Before the Palace of Oedipus.

Suppliants of all ages are seated round the altar at the palace doors, at their head a PRIEST OF ZEUS. To them enter OEDIPUS.

OEDIPUS

My children, latest born to Cadmus old,
Why sit ye here as suppliants, in your
hands
Branches of olive filleted with wool?
What means this reek of incense
everywhere,
And everywhere laments and litanies?
Children, it were not meet that I should
learn
From others, and am hither come, myself,
I Oedipus, your world-renowned king.
Ho! aged sire, whose venerable locks
Proclaim thee spokesman of this company,
Explain your mood and purport. Is it
dread
Of ill that moves you or a boon ye crave?
My zeal in your behalf ye cannot doubt;
Ruthless indeed were I and obdurate
If such petitioners as you I spurned.

PRIEST

Yea, Oedipus, my sovereign lord and king,
Thou seest how both extremes of age
besiege
Thy palace altars—fledglings hardly
winged,
and greybeards bowed with years; priests,
as am I
of Zeus, and these the flower of our
youth.

Meanwhile, the common folk, with
    wreathed boughs
Crowd our two market-places, or before
Both shrines of Pallas congregate, or
    where
Ismenus gives his oracles by fire.
For, as thou seest thyself, our ship of
    State,
Sore buffeted, can no more lift her head,
Foundered beneath a weltering surge of
    blood.
A blight is on our harvest in the ear,
A blight upon the grazing flocks and
    herds,
A blight on wives in travail; and withal
Armed with his blazing torch the God of
    Plague
Hath swooped upon our city emptying
The house of Cadmus, and the murky
    realm
Of Pluto is full fed with groans and tears.
Therefore, O King, here at thy hearth
    we sit,
I and these children; not as deeming thee
A new divinity, but the first of men;
First in the common accidents of life,
And first in visitations of the Gods.
Art thou not he who coming to the town
of Cadmus freed us from the tax we paid
To the fell songstress? Nor hadst thou
    received

Prompting from us or been by others
    schooled;
No, by a god inspired (so all men deem,
And testify) didst thou renew our life.
And now, O Oedipus, our peerless king,
All we thy votaries beseech thee, find
Some succor, whether by a voice from
    heaven
Whispered, or haply known by human wit.
Tried counselors, methinks, are aptest
    found[1]
To furnish for the future pregnant rede.
Upraise, O chief of men, upraise our
    State!
Look to thy laurels! for thy zeal of yore
Our country's savior thou art justly hailed:
O never may we thus record thy reign:—
"He raised us up only to cast us down."
Uplift us, build our city on a rock.
Thy happy star ascendant brought us luck,
O let it not decline! If thou wouldst rule
This land, as now thou reignest,
    better sure
To rule a peopled than a desert realm.
Nor battlements nor galleys aught avail,
If men to man and guards to guard them
    fail.

OEDIPUS

Ah! my poor children, known, ah, known
    too well,

The quest that brings you hither and your
    need.
Ye sicken all, well wot I, yet my pain,
How great soever yours, outtops it all.
Your sorrow touches each man severally,
Him and none other, but I grieve at once
Both for the general and myself and you.
Therefore ye rouse no sluggard from day-
    dreams.
Many, my children, are the tears I've wept,
And threaded many a maze of weary
    thought.
Thus pondering one clue of hope I
    caught,
And tracked it up; I have sent Menoeceus'
    son,
Creon, my consort's brother, to inquire
Of Pythian Phoebus at his Delphic shrine,
How I might save the State by act or word.
And now I reckon up the tale of days
Since he set forth, and marvel how he
    fares.
'Tis strange, this endless tarrying, passing
    strange.
But when he comes, then I were base
    indeed,
If I perform not all the god declares.

PRIEST
Thy words are well timed; even as thou
    speakest

That shouting tells me Creon is at hand.

OEDIPUS
O King Apollo! may his joyous looks
Be presage of the joyous news he brings!

PRIEST
As I surmise, 'tis welcome; else his head
Had scarce been crowned with berry-
    laden bays.

OEDIPUS
We soon shall know; he's now in earshot
    range.
[Enter CREON]
My royal cousin, say, Menoeceus' child,
What message hast thou brought us from
    the god?

CREON
Good news, for e'en intolerable ills,
Finding right issue, tend to naught but
    good.

OEDIPUS
How runs the oracle? thus far thy words
Give me no ground for confidence or fear.

CREON
If thou wouldst hear my message
    publicly,

I'll tell thee straight, or with thee pass
within.

OEDIPUS
Speak before all; the burden that I bear
Is more for these my subjects than myself.

CREON
Let me report then all the god declared.
King Phoebus bids us straitly extirpate
A fell pollution that infests the land,
And no more harbor an inveterate sore.

OEDIPUS
What expiation means he? What's amiss?

CREON
Banishment, or the shedding blood for
blood.
This stain of blood makes shipwreck of
our state.

OEDIPUS
Whom can he mean, the miscreant thus
denounced?

CREON
Before thou didst assume the helm of
State,
The sovereign of this land was Laius.

OEDIPUS
I heard as much, but never saw the man.

CREON
He fell; and now the god's command is
    plain:
Punish his takers-off, whoe'er they be.

OEDIPUS
Where are they? Where in the wide world
    to find
The far, faint traces of a bygone crime?

CREON
In this land, said the god; "who seeks shall
    find;
Who sits with folded hands or sleeps is
    blind."

OEDIPUS
Was he within his palace, or afield,
Or traveling, when Laius met his fate?

CREON
Abroad; he started, so he told us, bound
For Delphi, but he never thence returned.

OEDIPUS
Came there no news, no fellow-traveler
To give some clue that might be followed
    up?

CREON
But one escape, who flying for dear life,
Could tell of all he saw but one thing sure.

OEDIPUS
And what was that? One clue might lead
    us far,
With but a spark of hope to guide our
    quest.

CREON
Robbers, he told us, not one bandit but
A troop of knaves, attacked and murdered
    him.

OEDIPUS
Did any bandit dare so bold a stroke,
Unless indeed he were suborned from
    Thebes?

CREON
So 'twas surmised, but none was found to
    avenge
His murder mid the trouble that ensued.

OEDIPUS
What trouble can have hindered a full
    quest,
When royalty had fallen thus miserably?

CREON

The riddling Sphinx compelled us to let
  slide
The dim past and attend to instant needs.

OEDIPUS

Well, I will start afresh and once again
Make dark things clear. Right worthy the
  concern
Of Phoebus, worthy thine too, for the
  dead;
I also, as is meet, will lend my aid
To avenge this wrong to Thebes and to
  the god.
Not for some far-off kinsman, but myself,
Shall I expel this poison in the blood;
For whoso slew that king might have
  a mind
To strike me too with his assassin hand.
Therefore in righting him I serve myself.
Up, children, haste ye, quit these altar
  stairs,
Take hence your suppliant wands, go
  summon hither
The Theban commons. With the god's
  good help
Success is sure; 'tis ruin if we fail.
[Exeunt OEDIPUS and CREON]

PRIEST

Come, children, let us hence; these gra-
    cious words
Forestall the very purpose of our suit.
And may the god who sent this oracle
Save us withal and rid us of this pest.
[Exeunt PRIEST and SUPPLIANTS]

CHORUS

(Str. 1)

Sweet-voiced daughter of Zeus from thy
    gold-paved Pythian shrine
Wafted to Thebes divine,
What dost thou bring me? My soul is
    racked and shivers with fear.
(Healer of Delos, hear!)
Hast thou some pain unknown before,
Or with the circling years renewest a
    penance of yore?
Offspring of golden Hope, thou voice im-
    mortal, O tell me.

(Ant. 1)

First on Athene I call; O Zeus-born god-
    dess, defend!
Goddess and sister, befriend,
Artemis, Lady of Thebes, high-throned in
    the midst of our mart!
Lord of the death-winged dart!
Your threefold aid I crave
From death and ruin our city to save.

If in the days of old when we nigh had
    perished, ye drave
From our land the fiery plague, be near us
    now and defend us!

(Str. 2)
Ah me, what countless woes are mine!
All our host is in decline;
Weaponless my spirit lies.
Earth her gracious fruits denies;
Women wail in barren throes;
Life on life downstriken goes,
Swifter than the wind bird's flight,
Swifter than the Fire-God's might,
To the westering shores of Night.

(Ant. 2)
Wasted thus by death on death
All our city perisheth.
Corpses spread infection round;
None to tend or mourn is found.
Wailing on the altar stair
Wives and grandams rend the air—
Long-drawn moans and piercing cries
Blent with prayers and litanies.
Golden child of Zeus, O hear
Let thine angel face appear!

(Str. 3)
And grant that Ares whose hot breath I
    feel,

Though without targe or steel
He stalks, whose voice is as the battle
    shout,
May turn in sudden rout,
To the unharbored Thracian waters sped,
Or Amphitrite's bed.
For what night leaves undone,
Smit by the morrow's sun
Perisheth. Father Zeus, whose hand
Doth wield the lightning brand,
Slay him beneath thy levin bold, we pray,
Slay him, O slay!

(Ant. 3)
O that thine arrows too, Lycean King,
From that taut bow's gold string,
Might fly abroad, the champions of our
    rights;
Yea, and the flashing lights
Of Artemis, wherewith the huntress
    sweeps
Across the Lycian steeps.
Thee too I call with golden-snooded hair,
Whose name our land doth bear,
Bacchus to whom thy Maenads Evoe
    shout;
Come with thy bright torch, rout,
Blithe god whom we adore,
The god whom gods abhor.

[Enter OEDIPUS.]

OEDIPUS

Ye pray; 'tis well, but would ye hear my
    words
And heed them and apply the remedy,
Ye might perchance find comfort and
    relief.
Mind you, I speak as one who comes a
    stranger
To this report, no less than to the crime;
For how unaided could I track it far
Without a clue? Which lacking (for too late
Was I enrolled a citizen of Thebes)
This proclamation I address to all:—
Thebans, if any knows the man by whom
Laius, son of Labdacus, was slain,
I summon him to make clean shrift to me.
And if he shrinks, let him reflect that thus
Confessing he shall 'scape the capital
    charge;
For the worst penalty that shall befall him
Is banishment—unscathed he shall depart.
But if an alien from a foreign land
Be known to any as the murderer,
Let him who knows speak out, and he
    shall have
Due recompense from me and thanks to
    boot.
But if ye still keep silence, if through fear
For self or friends ye disregard my hest,
Hear what I then resolve; I lay my ban
On the assassin whosoe'er he be.

Let no man in this land, whereof I hold
The sovereign rule, harbor or speak
    to him;
Give him no part in prayer or sacrifice
Or lustral rites, but hound him from your
    homes.
For this is our defilement, so the god
Hath lately shown to me by oracles.
Thus as their champion I maintain the
    cause
Both of the god and of the murdered
    King.
And on the murderer this curse I lay
(On him and all the partners in his guilt):

Wretch, may he pine in utter
    wretchedness!
And for myself, if with my privity
He gain admittance to my hearth, I pray
The curse I laid on others fall on me.
See that ye give effect to all my hest,
For my sake and the god's and for our
    land,
A desert blasted by the wrath of heaven.
For, let alone the god's express command,
It were a scandal ye should leave unpurged
The murder of a great man and your king,
Nor track it home. And now that I am
    lord,
Successor to his throne, his bed, his wife,
(And had he not been frustrate in the hope

Of issue, common children of one womb
Had forced a closer bond twixt him
  and me,
But Fate swooped down upon him), there-
  fore I
His blood-avenger will maintain his cause
As though he were my sire, and leave no
  stone
Unturned to track the assassin or avenge
The son of Labdacus, of Polydore,
Of Cadmus, and Agenor first of the race.
And for the disobedient thus I pray:
May the gods send them neither timely
  fruits
Of earth, nor teeming increase of the
  womb,
But may they waste and pine, as now they
  waste,
Aye and worse stricken; but to all of you,
My loyal subjects who approve my acts,
May Justice, our ally, and all the gods
Be gracious and attend you evermore.

CHORUS
The oath thou profferest, sire, I take and
  swear.
I slew him not myself, nor can I name
The slayer. For the quest, 'twere well,
  methinks
That Phoebus, who proposed the riddle,
  himself

Should give the answer—who the murderer was.

OEDIPUS
Well argued; but no living man can hope
To force the gods to speak against their
  will.

CHORUS
May I then say what seems next best
  to me?

OEDIPUS
Aye, if there be a third best, tell it too.

CHORUS
My liege, if any man sees eye to eye
With our lord Phoebus, 'tis our prophet,
  lord
Teiresias; he of all men best might guide
A searcher of this matter to the light.

OEDIPUS
Here too my zeal has nothing lagged, for
  twice
At Creon's instance have I sent to
  fetch him,
And long I marvel why he is not here.

CHORUS
I mind me too of rumors long ago—

Mere gossip.

OEDIPUS
Tell them, I would fain know all.

CHORUS
'Twas said he fell by travelers.

OEDIPUS
So I heard,
But none has seen the man who saw him
    fall.

CHORUS
Well, if he knows what fear is, he will quail
And flee before the terror of thy curse.

OEDIPUS
Words scare not him who blenches not at
    deeds.

CHORUS
But here is one to arraign him. Lo, at
    length
They bring the god-inspired seer in whom
Above all other men is truth inborn.
[Enter TEIRESIAS, led by a boy.]

OEDIPUS
Teiresias, seer who comprehendest all,
Lore of the wise and hidden mysteries,

High things of heaven and low things of
    the earth,
Thou knowest, though thy blinded eyes see
    naught,
What plague infects our city; and we turn
To thee, O seer, our one defense and
    shield.
The purport of the answer that the God
Returned to us who sought his oracle,
The messengers have doubtless told
    thee—how
One course alone could rid us of the pest,
To find the murderers of Laius,
And slay them or expel them from the
    land.
Therefore begrudging neither augury
Nor other divination that is thine,
O save thyself, thy country, and thy king,
Save all from this defilement of blood
    shed.
On thee we rest. This is man's highest end,
To others' service all his powers to lend.

TEIRESIAS
Alas, alas, what misery to be wise
When wisdom profits nothing! This
    old lore
I had forgotten; else I were not here.

OEDIPUS

What ails thee? Why this melancholy
    mood?

TEIRESIAS

Let me go home; prevent me not;
    'twere best
That thou shouldst bear thy burden and I
    mine.

OEDIPUS

For shame! no true-born Theban patriot
Would thus withhold the word of
    prophecy.

TEIRESIAS

Thy words, O king, are wide of the mark,
    and I
For fear lest I too trip like thee...

OEDIPUS

Oh speak,
Withhold not, I adjure thee, if thou
    know'st,
Thy knowledge. We are all thy suppliants.

TEIRESIAS

Aye, for ye all are witless, but my voice
Will ne'er reveal my miseries—or thine.[2]

OEDIPUS

What then, thou knowest, and yet willst
    not speak!
Wouldst thou betray us and destroy the
    State?

TEIRESIAS

I will not vex myself nor thee. Why ask
Thus idly what from me thou shalt not
    learn?

OEDIPUS

Monster! thy silence would incense a flint.
Will nothing loose thy tongue? Can
    nothing melt thee,
Or shake thy dogged taciturnity?

TEIRESIAS

Thou blam'st my mood and seest not
    thine own
Wherewith thou art mated; no, thou
    taxest me.

OEDIPUS

And who could stay his choler when he
    heard
How insolently thou dost flout the State?

TEIRESIAS

Well, it will come what will, though I be
    mute.

OEDIPUS
Since come it must, thy duty is to tell me.

TEIRESIAS
I have no more to say; storm as thou willst,
And give the rein to all thy pent-up rage.

OEDIPUS
Yea, I am wroth, and will not stint my
    words,
But speak my whole mind. Thou methinks
    thou art he,
Who planned the crime, aye, and per-
    formed it too,
All save the assassination; and if thou
Hadst not been blind, I had been sworn
    to boot
That thou alone didst do the bloody deed.

TEIRESIAS
Is it so? Then I charge thee to abide
By thine own proclamation; from this day
Speak not to these or me. Thou art
    the man,
Thou the accursed polluter of this land.

OEDIPUS
Vile slanderer, thou blurtest forth these
    taunts,
And think'st forsooth as seer to go scot
    free.

TEIRESIAS
Yea, I am free, strong in the strength of
     truth.

OEDIPUS
Who was thy teacher? not methinks
     thy art.

TEIRESIAS
Thou, goading me against my will to
     speak.

OEDIPUS
What speech? repeat it and resolve my
     doubt.

TEIRESIAS
Didst miss my sense wouldst thou goad
     me on?

OEDIPUS
I but half caught thy meaning; say it
     again.

TEIRESIAS
I say thou art the murderer of the man
Whose murderer thou pursuest.

OEDIPUS
Thou shalt rue it
Twice to repeat so gross a calumny.

TEIRESIAS
Must I say more to aggravate thy rage?

OEDIPUS
Say all thou wilt; it will be but waste of
    breath.

TEIRESIAS
I say thou livest with thy nearest kin
In infamy, unwitting in thy shame.

OEDIPUS
Think'st thou for aye unscathed to wag thy
    tongue?

TEIRESIAS
Yea, if the might of truth can aught
    prevail.
OEDIPUS
With other men, but not with thee,
    for thou
In ear, wit, eye, in everything art blind.

TEIRESIAS
Poor fool to utter gibes at me which all
Here present will cast back on thee ere
    long.

OEDIPUS
Offspring of endless Night, thou hast no
    power

O'er me or any man who sees the sun.

TEIRESIAS
No, for thy weird is not to fall by me.
I leave to Apollo what concerns the god.

OEDIPUS
Is this a plot of Creon, or thine own?

TEIRESIAS
Not Creon, thou thyself art thine own
    bane.

OEDIPUS
O wealth and empiry and skill by skill
Outwitted in the battlefield of life,
What spite and envy follow in your train!
See, for this crown the State conferred
    on me.
A gift, a thing I sought not, for this crown
The trusty Creon, my familiar friend,
Hath lain in wait to oust me and suborned
This mountebank, this juggling charlatan,
This tricksy beggar-priest, for gain alone
Keen-eyed, but in his proper art stone-
    blind.
Say, sirrah, hast thou ever proved thyself
A prophet? When the riddling Sphinx
    was here
Why hadst thou no deliverance for this
    folk?

And yet the riddle was not to be solved
By guess-work but required the prophet's
    art;
Wherein thou wast found lacking; neither
    birds
Nor sign from heaven helped thee, but I
    came,
The simple Oedipus; I stopped her mouth
By mother wit, untaught of auguries.
This is the man whom thou wouldst un-
    dermine,
In hope to reign with Creon in my stead.
Methinks that thou and thine abettor soon
Will rue your plot to drive the scapegoat
    out.
Thank thy grey hairs that thou hast still to
    learn
What chastisement such arrogance
    deserves.

CHORUS
To us it seems that both the seer and thou,
O Oedipus, have spoken angry words.
This is no time to wrangle but consult
How best we may fulfill the oracle.

TEIRESIAS
King as thou art, free speech at least
    is mine
To make reply; in this I am thy peer.
I own no lord but Loxias; him I serve

And ne'er can stand enrolled as Creon's
    man.
Thus then I answer: since thou hast not
    spared
To twit me with my blindness—thou hast
    eyes,
Yet see'st not in what misery thou art
    fallen,
Nor where thou dwellest nor with whom
    for mate.
Dost know thy lineage? Nay, thou know'st
    it not,
And all unwitting art a double foe
To thine own kin, the living and the dead;
Aye and the dogging curse of mother
    and sire
One day shall drive thee, like a two-edged
    sword,
Beyond our borders, and the eyes that now
See clear shall henceforward endless night.
Ah whither shall thy bitter cry not reach,
What crag in all Cithaeron but shall then
Reverberate thy wail, when thou hast
    found
With what a hymeneal thou wast borne
Home, but to no fair haven, on the gale!
Aye, and a flood of ills thou guessest not
Shall set thyself and children in one line.
Flout then both Creon and my words,
    for none

Of mortals shall be striken worse than
    thou.

OEDIPUS
Must I endure this fellow's insolence?
A murrain on thee! Get thee hence!
    Begone
Avaunt! and never cross my threshold
    more.

TEIRESIAS
I ne'er had come hadst thou not
    bidden me.

OEDIPUS
I know not thou wouldst utter folly, else
Long hadst thou waited to be summoned
    here.

TEIRESIAS
Such am I—as it seems to thee a fool,
But to the parents who begat thee, wise.

OEDIPUS
What sayest thou—"parents"? Who begat
    me, speak?

TEIRESIAS
This day shall be thy birth-day, and thy
    grave.

OEDIPUS
Thou lov'st to speak in riddles and dark
    words.

TEIRESIAS
In reading riddles who so skilled as thou?

OEDIPUS
Twit me with that wherein my greatness
    lies.

TEIRESIAS
And yet this very greatness proved thy
    bane.

OEDIPUS
No matter if I saved the commonwealth.

TEIRESIAS
'Tis time I left thee. Come, boy, take me
    home.

OEDIPUS
Aye, take him quickly, for his presence irks
And lets me; gone, thou canst not plague
    me more.

TEIRESIAS
I go, but first will tell thee why I came.
Thy frown I dread not, for thou canst not
    harm me.

Hear then: this man whom thou hast
    sought to arrest
With threats and warrants this long while,
    the wretch
Who murdered Laius—that man is here.
He passes for an alien in the land
But soon shall prove a Theban, native
    born.
And yet his fortune brings him little joy;
For blind of seeing, clad in beggar's weeds,
For purple robes, and leaning on his staff,
To a strange land he soon shall grope
    his way.
And of the children, inmates of his home,
He shall be proved the brother and the
    sire,
Of her who bare him son and husband
    both,
Co-partner, and assassin of his sire.
Go in and ponder this, and if thou find
That I have missed the mark, henceforth
    declare
I have no wit nor skill in prophecy.
[Exeunt TEIRESIAS and OEDIPUS]

CHORUS
(Str. 1)
Who is he by voice immortal named from
    Pythia's rocky cell,
Doer of foul deeds of bloodshed, horrors
    that no tongue can tell?

A foot for flight he needs
Fleeter than storm-swift steeds,
For on his heels doth follow,
Armed with the lightnings of his Sire,
    Apollo.
Like sleuth-hounds too
The Fates pursue.

(Ant. 1)
Yea, but now flashed forth the summons
    from Parnassus' snowy peak,
"Near and far the undiscovered doer of
    this murder seek!"
Now like a sullen bull he roves
Through forest brakes and upland groves,
And vainly seeks to fly
The doom that ever nigh
Flits o'er his head,
Still by the avenging Phoebus sped,
The voice divine,
From Earth's mid shrine.
(Str. 2)
Sore perplexed am I by the words of the
    master seer.
Are they true, are they false? I know not
    and bridle my tongue for
fear,
Fluttered with vague surmise; nor present
    nor future is clear.
Quarrel of ancient date or in days still
    near know I none

Twixt the Labdacidan house and our ruler,
    Polybus' son.
Proof is there none: how then can I chal-
    lenge our King's good name,
How in a blood-feud join for an untracked
    deed of shame?

(Ant. 2)
All wise are Zeus and Apollo, and nothing
    is hid from their ken;
They are gods; and in wits a man may sur-
    pass his fellow men;
But that a mortal seer knows more than I
    know—where
Hath this been proven? Or how without
    sign assured, can I blame
Him who saved our State when the winged
    songstress came,
Tested and tried in the light of us all, like
    gold assayed?
How can I now assent when a crime is on
    Oedipus laid?

CREON
Friends, countrymen, I learn King
    Oedipus
Hath laid against me a most grievous
    charge,
And come to you protesting. If he deems
That I have harmed or injured him in
    aught

By word or deed in this our present
    trouble,
I care not to prolong the span of life,
Thus ill-reputed; for the calumny
Hits not a single blot, but blasts my name,
If by the general voice I am denounced
False to the State and false by you my
    friends.

CHORUS
This taunt, it well may be, was blurted out
In petulance, not spoken advisedly.

CREON
Did any dare pretend that it was I
Prompted the seer to utter a forged
    charge?

CHORUS
Such things were said; with what intent I
    know not.

CREON
Were not his wits and vision all astray
When upon me he fixed this monstrous
    charge?

CHORUS
I know not; to my sovereign's acts I am
    blind.
But lo, he comes to answer for himself.

[Enter OEDIPUS.]

OEDIPUS

Sirrah, what mak'st thou here? Dost thou
    presume
To approach my doors, thou brazen-faced
    rogue,
My murderer and the filcher of my
    crown?
Come, answer this, didst thou detect in me
Some touch of cowardice or witlessness,
That made thee undertake this enterprise?
I seemed forsooth too simple to perceive
The serpent stealing on me in the dark,
Or else too weak to scotch it when I saw.
This thou art witless seeking to possess
Without a following or friends the crown,
A prize that followers and wealth
    must win.

CREON

Attend me. Thou hast spoken, 'tis my turn
To make reply. Then having heard me,
    judge.

OEDIPUS

Thou art glib of tongue, but I am slow to
    learn
Of thee; I know too well thy venomous
    hate.

CREON
First I would argue out this very point.

OEDIPUS
O argue not that thou art not a rogue.

CREON
If thou dost count a virtue stubbornness,
Unschooled by reason, thou art much
    astray.

OEDIPUS
If thou dost hold a kinsman may be
    wronged,
And no pains follow, thou art much to
    seek.

CREON
Therein thou judgest rightly, but this
    wrong
That thou allegest—tell me what it is.

OEDIPUS
Didst thou or didst thou not advise that I
Should call the priest?

CREON
Yes, and I stand to it.

OEDIPUS
Tell me how long is it since Laius...

CREON
Since Laius...? I follow not thy drift.

OEDIPUS
By violent hands was spirited away.

CREON
In the dim past, a many years agone.

OEDIPUS
Did the same prophet then pursue his
    craft?

CREON
Yes, skilled as now and in no less repute.

OEDIPUS
Did he at that time ever glance at me?

CREON
Not to my knowledge, not when I was by.

OEDIPUS
But was no search and inquisition made?

CREON
Surely full quest was made, but nothing
    learnt.

OEDIPUS
Why failed the seer to tell his story then?

CREON
I know not, and not knowing hold my
    tongue.

OEDIPUS
This much thou knowest and canst surely
    tell.

CREON
What's mean'st thou? All I know I will
    declare.

OEDIPUS
But for thy prompting never had the seer
Ascribed to me the death of Laius.

CREON
If so he thou knowest best; but I
Would put thee to the question in my turn.

OEDIPUS
Question and prove me murderer if thou
    canst.

CREON
Then let me ask thee, didst thou wed my
    sister?

OEDIPUS
A fact so plain I cannot well deny.

CREON
And as thy consort queen she shares the
    throne?

OEDIPUS
I grant her freely all her heart desires.

CREON
And with you twain I share the triple rule?

OEDIPUS
Yea, and it is that proves thee a false
    friend.

CREON
Not so, if thou wouldst reason with thyself,
As I with myself. First, I bid thee think,
Would any mortal choose a troubled reign
Of terrors rather than secure repose,
If the same power were given him? As
    for me,
I have no natural craving for the name
Of king, preferring to do kingly deeds,
And so thinks every sober-minded man.
Now all my needs are satisfied through
    thee,
And I have naught to fear; but were I king,
My acts would oft run counter to my will.
How could a title then have charms for me
Above the sweets of boundless influence?
I am not so infatuate as to grasp

The shadow when I hold the substance
    fast.
Now all men cry me Godspeed! wish me
    well,
And every suitor seeks to gain my ear,
If he would hope to win a grace from thee.
Why should I leave the better, choose the
    worse?
That were sheer madness, and I am
    not mad.
No such ambition ever tempted me,
Nor would I have a share in such intrigue.
And if thou doubt me, first to Delphi go,
There ascertain if my report was true
Of the god's answer; next investigate
If with the seer I plotted or conspired,
And if it prove so, sentence me to death,
Not by thy voice alone, but mine and
    thine.
But O condemn me not, without appeal,
On bare suspicion. 'Tis not right to
    adjudge
Bad men at random good, or good
    men bad.
I would as lief a man should cast away
The thing he counts most precious, his
    own life,
As spurn a true friend. Thou wilt learn
    in time
The truth, for time alone reveals the just;
A villain is detected in a day.

CHORUS
To one who walketh warily his words
Commend themselves; swift counsels are
    not sure.

OEDIPUS
When with swift strides the stealthy plotter
    stalks
I must be quick too with my counterplot.
To wait his onset passively, for him
Is sure success, for me assured defeat.

CREON
What then's thy will? To banish me the
    land?

OEDIPUS
I would not have thee banished, no, but
    dead,
That men may mark the wages envy reaps.

CREON
I see thou wilt not yield, nor credit me.

OEDIPUS
[None but a fool would credit such as
    thou.][3]

CREON
Thou art not wise.

OEDIPUS
Wise for myself at least.

CREON
Why not for me too?

OEDIPUS
Why for such a knave?

CREON
Suppose thou lackest sense.

OEDIPUS
Yet kings must rule.

CREON
Not if they rule ill.

OEDIPUS
Oh my Thebans, hear him!

CREON
Thy Thebans? am not I a Theban too?

CHORUS
Cease, princes; lo there comes, and none
        too soon,
Jocasta from the palace. Who so fit
As peacemaker to reconcile your feud?
[Enter JOCASTA.]

JOCASTA
Misguided princes, why have ye upraised
This wordy wrangle? Are ye not ashamed,
While the whole land lies striken, thus to
        voice
Your private injuries? Go in, my lord;
Go home, my brother, and forebear
        to make
A public scandal of a petty grief.

CREON
My royal sister, Oedipus, thy lord,
Hath bid me choose (O dread alternative!)
An outlaw's exile or a felon's death.

OEDIPUS
Yes, lady; I have caught him practicing
Against my royal person his vile arts.

CREON
May I ne'er speed but die accursed, if I
In any way am guilty of this charge.

JOCASTA
Believe him, I adjure thee, Oedipus,
First for his solemn oath's sake, then for
        mine,
And for thine elders' sake who wait on
        thee.

CHORUS
(Str. 1)
Hearken, King, reflect, we pray thee, but
    not stubborn but relent.

OEDIPUS
Say to what should I consent?

CHORUS
Respect a man whose probity and troth
Are known to all and now confirmed by
    oath.

OEDIPUS
Dost know what grace thou cravest?

CHORUS
Yea, I know.

OEDIPUS
Declare it then and make thy meaning
    plain.

CHORUS
Brand not a friend whom babbling
    tongues assail;
Let not suspicion 'gainst his oath prevail.

OEDIPUS
Bethink you that in seeking this ye seek
In very sooth my death or banishment?

CHORUS

No, by the leader of the host divine!
(Str. 2)
Witness, thou Sun, such thought was never
    mine,
Unblest, unfriended may I perish,
If ever I such wish did cherish!
But O my heart is desolate
Musing on our striken State,
Doubly fall'n should discord grow
Twixt you twain, to crown our woe.

OEDIPUS

Well, let him go, no matter what it
    cost me,
Or certain death or shameful banishment,
For your sake I relent, not his; and him,
Where'er he be, my heart shall still abhor.

CREON

Thou art as sullen in thy yielding mood
As in thine anger thou wast truculent.
Such tempers justly plague themselves the
    most.

OEDIPUS

Leave me in peace and get thee gone.

CREON

I go,
By thee misjudged, but justified by these.

[Exeunt CREON]

CHORUS
(Ant. 1)
Lady, lead indoors thy consort; wherefore
　　longer here delay?

JOCASTA
Tell me first how rose the fray.

CHORUS
Rumors bred unjust suspicious and injus-
　　tice rankles sore.

JOCASTA
Were both at fault?

CHORUS
Both.

JOCASTA
What was the tale?

CHORUS
Ask me no more. The land is sore dis-
　　tressed;
'Twere better sleeping ills to leave at rest.

OEDIPUS
Strange counsel, friend! I know thou
　　mean'st me well,

And yet would'st mitigate and blunt my
    zeal.

CHORUS
(Ant. 2)
King, I say it once again,
Witless were I proved, insane,
If I lightly put away
Thee my country's prop and stay,
Pilot who, in danger sought,
To a quiet haven brought
Our distracted State; and now
Who can guide us right but thou?

JOCASTA
Let me too, I adjure thee, know, O king,
What cause has stirred this unrelenting
    wrath.

OEDIPUS
I will, for thou art more to me than these.
Lady, the cause is Creon and his plots.

JOCASTA
But what provoked the quarrel? make this
    clear.

OEDIPUS
He points me out as Laius' murderer.

JOCASTA

Of his own knowledge or upon report?

OEDIPUS

He is too cunning to commit himself,
And makes a mouthpiece of a knavish
    seer.

JOCASTA

Then thou mayest ease thy conscience on
    that score.
Listen and I'll convince thee that no man
Hath scot or lot in the prophetic art.
Here is the proof in brief. An oracle
Once came to Laius (I will not say
'Twas from the Delphic god himself,
    but from
His ministers) declaring he was doomed
To perish by the hand of his own son,
A child that should be born to him by me.
Now Laius—so at least report affirmed—
Was murdered on a day by highwaymen,
No natives, at a spot where three roads
    meet.
As for the child, it was but three days old,
When Laius, its ankles pierced and pinned
Together, gave it to be cast away
By others on the trackless mountain side.
So then Apollo brought it not to pass
The child should be his father's murderer,
Or the dread terror find accomplishment,

And Laius be slain by his own son.
Such was the prophet's horoscope. O king,
Regard it not. Whate'er the god deems fit
To search, himself unaided will reveal.

OEDIPUS
What memories, what wild tumult of
        the soul
Came o'er me, lady, as I heard thee speak!

JOCASTA
What mean'st thou? What has shocked
        and startled thee?

OEDIPUS
Methought I heard thee say that Laius
Was murdered at the meeting of three
        roads.

JOCASTA
So ran the story that is current still.

OEDIPUS
Where did this happen? Dost thou know
        the place?

JOCASTA
Phocis the land is called; the spot is where
Branch roads from Delphi and from
        Daulis meet.

OEDIPUS
And how long is it since these things
    befell?

JOCASTA
'Twas but a brief while were thou wast
    proclaimed
Our country's ruler that the news was
    brought.

OEDIPUS
O Zeus, what hast thou willed to do
    with me!

JOCASTA
What is it, Oedipus, that moves thee so?

OEDIPUS
Ask me not yet; tell me the build and
    height
Of Laius? Was he still in manhood's
    prime?

JOCASTA
Tall was he, and his hair was lightly strewn
With silver; and not unlike thee in form.

OEDIPUS
O woe is me! Methinks unwittingly
I laid but now a dread curse on myself.

JOCASTA
What say'st thou? When I look upon thee,
    my king,
I tremble.

OEDIPUS
'Tis a dread presentiment
That in the end the seer will prove not
    blind.
One further question to resolve my doubt.

JOCASTA
I quail; but ask, and I will answer all.

OEDIPUS
Had he but few attendants or a train
Of armed retainers with him, like a
    prince?

JOCASTA
They were but five in all, and one of them
A herald; Laius in a mule-car rode.

OEDIPUS
Alas! 'tis clear as noonday now. But say,
Lady, who carried this report to Thebes?

JOCASTA
A serf, the sole survivor who returned.

OEDIPUS

Haply he is at hand or in the house?

JOCASTA

No, for as soon as he returned and found
Thee reigning in the stead of Laius slain,
He clasped my hand and supplicated me
To send him to the alps and pastures,
    where
He might be farthest from the sight of
    Thebes.
And so I sent him. 'Twas an honest slave
And well deserved some better rec-
    ompense.

OEDIPUS

Fetch him at once. I fain would see
    the man.

JOCASTA

He shall be brought; but wherefore
    summon him?

OEDIPUS

Lady, I fear my tongue has overrun
Discretion; therefore I would question
    him.

JOCASTA

Well, he shall come, but may not I too
    claim

To share the burden of thy heart, my king?

OEDIPUS
And thou shalt not be frustrate of thy
    wish.
Now my imaginings have gone so far.
Who has a higher claim that thou to hear
My tale of dire adventures? Listen then.
My sire was Polybus of Corinth, and
My mother Merope, a Dorian;
And I was held the foremost citizen,
Till a strange thing befell me, strange
    indeed,
Yet scarce deserving all the heat it stirred.
A roisterer at some banquet, flown with
    wine,
Shouted "Thou art not true son of thy
    sire."
It irked me, but I stomached for the nonce
The insult; on the morrow I sought out
My mother and my sire and questioned
    them.
They were indignant at the random slur
Cast on my parentage and did their best
To comfort me, but still the venomed barb
Rankled, for still the scandal spread and
    grew.
So privily without their leave I went
To Delphi, and Apollo sent me back
Baulked of the knowledge that I came to
    seek.

But other grievous things he prophesied,
Woes, lamentations, mourning, portents
    dire;
To wit I should defile my mother's bed
And raise up seed too loathsome to
    behold,
And slay the father from whose loins I
    sprang.
Then, lady,—thou shalt hear the very
    truth—
As I drew near the triple-branching roads,
A herald met me and a man who sat
In a car drawn by colts—as in thy tale—
The man in front and the old man himself
Threatened to thrust me rudely from the
    path,
Then jostled by the charioteer in wrath
I struck him, and the old man, seeing this,
Watched till I passed and from his car
    brought down
Full on my head the double-pointed goad.
Yet was I quits with him and more; one
    stroke
Of my good staff sufficed to fling him
    clean
Out of the chariot seat and laid him
    prone.
And so I slew them every one. But if
Betwixt this stranger there was aught in
    common
With Laius, who more miserable than I,

What mortal could you find more god-
    abhorred?
Wretch whom no sojourner, no citizen
May harbor or address, whom all are
    bound
To harry from their homes. And this same
    curse
Was laid on me, and laid by none but me.
Yea with these hands all gory I pollute
The bed of him I slew. Say, am I vile?
Am I not utterly unclean, a wretch
Doomed to be banished, and in ban-
    ishment
Forgo the sight of all my dearest ones,
And never tread again my native earth;
Or else to wed my mother and slay my
    sire,
Polybus, who begat me and upreared?
If one should say, this is the handiwork
Of some inhuman power, who could
    blame
His judgment? But, ye pure and awful
    gods,
Forbid, forbid that I should see that day!
May I be blotted out from living men
Ere such a plague spot set on me its brand!

CHORUS
We too, O king, are troubled; but till thou
Hast questioned the survivor, still hope on.

OEDIPUS

My hope is faint, but still enough survives
To bid me bide the coming of this herd.

JOCASTA

Suppose him here, what wouldst thou
    learn of him?

OEDIPUS

I'll tell thee, lady; if his tale agrees
With thine, I shall have 'scaped calamity.

JOCASTA

And what of special import did I say?

OEDIPUS

In thy report of what the herdsman said
Laius was slain by robbers; now if he
Still speaks of robbers, not a robber, I
Slew him not; "one" with "many" cannot
    square.
But if he says one lonely wayfarer,
The last link wanting to my guilt is forged.

JOCASTA

Well, rest assured, his tale ran thus at first,
Nor can he now retract what then he said;
Not I alone but all our townsfolk heard it.
E'en should he vary somewhat in his story,
He cannot make the death of Laius
In any wise jump with the oracle.

For Loxias said expressly he was doomed
To die by my child's hand, but he, poor
     babe,
He shed no blood, but perished first
     himself.
So much for divination. Henceforth I
Will look for signs neither to right nor left.

OEDIPUS
Thou reasonest well. Still I would have
     thee send
And fetch the bondsman hither. See to it.

JOCASTA
That will I straightway. Come, let us
     within.
I would do nothing that my lord mislikes.
[Exeunt OEDIPUS and JOCASTA]

CHORUS
(Str. 1)
My lot be still to lead
The life of innocence and fly
Irreverence in word or deed,
To follow still those laws ordained on high
Whose birthplace is the bright ethereal sky
No mortal birth they own,
Olympus their progenitor alone:
Ne'er shall they slumber in oblivion cold,
The god in them is strong and grows
     not old.

(Ant. 1)

Of insolence is bred
The tyrant; insolence full blown,
With empty riches surfeited,
Scales the precipitous height and grasps
    the throne.
Then topples o'er and lies in ruin prone;
No foothold on that dizzy steep.
But O may Heaven the true patriot keep
Who burns with emulous zeal to serve the
    State.
God is my help and hope, on him I wait.

(Str. 2)

But the proud sinner, or in word or deed,
That will not Justice heed,
Nor reverence the shrine
Of images divine,
Perdition seize his vain imaginings,
If, urged by greed profane,
He grasps at ill-got gain,
And lays an impious hand on holiest
    things.
Who when such deeds are done
Can hope heaven's bolts to shun?
If sin like this to honor can aspire,
Why dance I still and lead the sacred
    choir?

(Ant. 2)

No more I'll seek earth's central oracle,

Or Abae's hallowed cell,
Nor to Olympia bring
My votive offering.
If before all God's truth be not bade plain.
O Zeus, reveal thy might,
King, if thou'rt named aright
Omnipotent, all-seeing, as of old;
For Laius is forgot;
His weird, men heed it not;
Apollo is forsook and faith grows cold.
[Enter JOCASTA.]

JOCASTA
My lords, ye look amazed to see your
    queen
With wreaths and gifts of incense in her
    hands.
I had a mind to visit the high shrines,
For Oedipus is overwrought, alarmed
With terrors manifold. He will not use
His past experience, like a man of sense,
To judge the present need, but lends
    an ear
To any croaker if he augurs ill.
Since then my counsels naught avail,
    I turn
To thee, our present help in time of
    trouble,
Apollo, Lord Lycean, and to thee
My prayers and supplications here I
    bring.

Lighten us, lord, and cleanse us from this
    curse!
For now we all are cowed like mariners
Who see their helmsman dumbstruck in
    the storm.

[Enter Corinthian MESSENGER.]

MESSENGER
My masters, tell me where the palace is
Of Oedipus; or better, where's the king.

CHORUS
Here is the palace and he bides within;
This is his queen the mother of his
    children.

MESSENGER
All happiness attend her and the house,
Blessed is her husband and her marriage-
    bed.

JOCASTA
My greetings to thee, stranger; thy fair
    words
Deserve a like response. But tell me why
Thou comest—what thy need or what thy
    news.

MESSENGER
Good for thy consort and the royal house.

JOCASTA

What may it be? Whose messenger art
    thou?

MESSENGER

The Isthmian commons have resolved
    to make
Thy husband king—so 'twas reported
    there.

JOCASTA

What! is not aged Polybus still king?

MESSENGER

No, verily; he's dead and in his grave.

JOCASTA

What! is he dead, the sire of Oedipus?

MESSENGER

If I speak falsely, may I die myself.

JOCASTA

Quick, maiden, bear these tidings to my
    lord.
Ye god-sent oracles, where stand ye now!
This is the man whom Oedipus long
    shunned,
In dread to prove his murderer; and now
He dies in nature's course, not by his
    hand.

[Enter OEDIPUS.]

OEDIPUS
My wife, my queen, Jocasta, why hast thou
Summoned me from my palace?

JOCASTA
Hear this man,
And as thou hearest judge what has
    become
Of all those awe-inspiring oracles.

OEDIPUS
Who is this man, and what his news
    for me?

JOCASTA
He comes from Corinth and his message
    this:
Thy father Polybus hath passed away.

OEDIPUS
What? let me have it, stranger, from thy
    mouth.

MESSENGER
If I must first make plain beyond a doubt
My message, know that Polybus is dead.

OEDIPUS
By treachery, or by sickness visited?

MESSENGER
One touch will send an old man to his rest.

OEDIPUS
So of some malady he died, poor man.

MESSENGER
Yes, having measured the full span of
    years.

OEDIPUS
Out on it, lady! why should one regard
The Pythian hearth or birds that scream i'
    the air?
Did they not point at me as doomed
    to slay
My father? but he's dead and in his grave
And here am I who ne'er unsheathed a
    sword;
Unless the longing for his absent son
Killed him and so I slew him in a sense.
But, as they stand, the oracles are dead—
Dust, ashes, nothing, dead as Polybus.

JOCASTA
Say, did not I foretell this long ago?

OEDIPUS
Thou didst: but I was misled by my fear.

JOCASTA
Then let I no more weigh upon thy soul.

OEDIPUS
Must I not fear my mother's marriage bed.

JOCASTA
Why should a mortal man, the sport of
      chance,
With no assured foreknowledge, be afraid?
Best live a careless life from hand to
      mouth.
This wedlock with thy mother fear not
      thou.
How oft it chances that in dreams a man
Has wed his mother! He who least regards
Such brainsick phantasies lives most at
      ease.

OEDIPUS
I should have shared in full thy confidence,
Were not my mother living; since she lives
Though half convinced I still must live in
      dread.

JOCASTA
And yet thy sire's death lights out darkness
      much.

OEDIPUS
Much, but my fear is touching her who
    lives.

MESSENGER
Who may this woman be whom thus you
    fear?

OEDIPUS
Merope, stranger, wife of Polybus.

MESSENGER
And what of her can cause you any fear?

OEDIPUS
A heaven-sent oracle of dread import.

MESSENGER
A mystery, or may a stranger hear it?

OEDIPUS
Aye, 'tis no secret. Loxias once foretold
That I should mate with mine own
    mother, and shed
With my own hands the blood of my own
    sire.
Hence Corinth was for many a year to me
A home distant; and I trove abroad,
But missed the sweetest sight, my parents'
    face.

MESSENGER
Was this the fear that exiled thee from
    home?

OEDIPUS
Yea, and the dread of slaying my own sire.

MESSENGER
Why, since I came to give thee pleasure,
    King,
Have I not rid thee of this second fear?

OEDIPUS
Well, thou shalt have due guerdon for thy
    pains.

MESSENGER
Well, I confess what chiefly made me come
Was hope to profit by thy coming home.

OEDIPUS
Nay, I will ne'er go near my parents more.

MESSENGER
My son, 'tis plain, thou know'st not what
    thou doest.

OEDIPUS
How so, old man? For heaven's sake tell
    me all.

MESSENGER
If this is why thou dreadest to return.

OEDIPUS
Yea, lest the god's word be fulfilled in me.

MESSENGER
Lest through thy parents thou shouldst be
    accursed?

OEDIPUS
This and none other is my constant dread.

MESSENGER
Dost thou not know thy fears are baseless
    all?

OEDIPUS
How baseless, if I am their very son?

MESSENGER
Since Polybus was naught to thee in blood.

OEDIPUS
What say'st thou? was not Polybus my sire?

MESSENGER
As much thy sire as I am, and no more.

OEDIPUS
My sire no more to me than one who is
    naught?

MESSENGER
Since I begat thee not, no more did he.

OEDIPUS
What reason had he then to call me son?

MESSENGER
Know that he took thee from my hands, a
    gift.

OEDIPUS
Yet, if no child of his, he loved me well.

MESSENGER
A childless man till then, he warmed to
    thee.

OEDIPUS
A foundling or a purchased slave, this
    child?

MESSENGER
I found thee in Cithaeron's wooded glens.

OEDIPUS
What led thee to explore those upland
    glades?

MESSENGER
My business was to tend the mountain
    flocks.

OEDIPUS
A vagrant shepherd journeying for hire?

MESSENGER
True, but thy savior in that hour, my son.

OEDIPUS
My savior? from what harm? what ailed
    me then?

MESSENGER
Those ankle joints are evidence enow.

OEDIPUS
Ah, why remind me of that ancient sore?

MESSENGER
I loosed the pin that riveted thy feet.

OEDIPUS
Yes, from my cradle that dread brand I
    bore.

MESSENGER
Whence thou deriv'st the name that still is
    thine.

OEDIPUS
Who did it? I adjure thee, tell me who
Say, was it father, mother?

MESSENGER
I know not.
The man from whom I had thee may
    know more.

OEDIPUS
What, did another find me, not thyself?

MESSENGER
Not I; another shepherd gave thee me.

OEDIPUS
Who was he? Would'st thou know again
    the man?

MESSENGER
He passed indeed for one of Laius' house.

OEDIPUS
The king who ruled the country long ago?

MESSENGER
The same: he was a herdsman of the king.

OEDIPUS
And is he living still for me to see him?

MESSENGER

His fellow-countrymen should best know
    that.

OEDIPUS

Doth any bystander among you know
The herd he speaks of, or by seeing him
Afield or in the city? answer straight!
The hour hath come to clear this business
    up.

CHORUS

Methinks he means none other than
    the hind
Whom thou anon wert fain to see; but that
Our queen Jocasta best of all could tell.

OEDIPUS

Madam, dost know the man we sent to
    fetch?
Is the same of whom the stranger speaks?

JOCASTA

Who is the man? What matter? Let it be.
'Twere waste of thought to weigh such idle
    words.

OEDIPUS

No, with such guiding clues I cannot fail
To bring to light the secret of my birth.

JOCASTA
Oh, as thou carest for thy life, give o'er
This quest. Enough the anguish I endure.

OEDIPUS
Be of good cheer; though I be proved
    the son
Of a bondwoman, aye, through three
    descents
Triply a slave, thy honor is unsmirched.

JOCASTA
Yet humor me, I pray thee; do not this.

OEDIPUS
I cannot; I must probe this matter home.

JOCASTA
'Tis for thy sake I advise thee for the best.

OEDIPUS
I grow impatient of this best advice.

JOCASTA
Ah mayst thou ne'er discover who
    thou art!

OEDIPUS
Go, fetch me here the herd, and leave yon
    woman
To glory in her pride of ancestry.

JOCASTA

O woe is thee, poor wretch! With that
    last word
I leave thee, henceforth silent evermore.
[Exit JOCASTA]

CHORUS

Why, Oedipus, why stung with passionate
    grief
Hath the queen thus departed? Much
    I fear
From this dead calm will burst a storm of
    woes.

OEDIPUS

Let the storm burst, my fixed resolve still
    holds,
To learn my lineage, be it ne'er so low.
It may be she with all a woman's pride
Thinks scorn of my base parentage. But I
Who rank myself as Fortune's favorite
    child,
The giver of good gifts, shall not be
    shamed.
She is my mother and the changing moons
My brethren, and with them I wax and
    wane.
Thus sprung why should I fear to trace my
    birth?
Nothing can make me other than I am.

CHORUS
(Str.)
If my soul prophetic err not, if my wisdom
    aught avail,
Thee, Cithaeron, I shall hail,
As the nurse and foster-mother of our
    Oedipus shall greet
Ere tomorrow's full moon rises, and exalt
    thee as is meet.
Dance and song shall hymn thy praises,
    lover of our royal race.
Phoebus, may my words find grace!

(Ant.)
Child, who bare thee, nymph or goddess?
    sure thy sure was more than
man,
Haply the hill-roamer Pan.
Of did Loxias beget thee, for he haunts
    the upland wold;
Or Cyllene's lord, or Bacchus, dweller on
    the hilltops cold?
Did some Heliconian Oread give him
    thee, a new-born joy?
Nymphs with whom he love to toy?

OEDIPUS
Elders, if I, who never yet before
Have met the man, may make a guess,
    methinks

I see the herdsman who we long have
    sought;
His time-worn aspect matches with the
    years
Of yonder aged messenger; besides   .
I seem to recognize the men who
    bring him
As servants of my own. But you,
    perchance,
Having in past days known or seen the
    herd,
May better by sure knowledge my surmise.

CHORUS
I recognize him; one of Laius' house;
A simple hind, but true as any man.
[Enter HERDSMAN.]

OEDIPUS
Corinthian, stranger, I address thee first,
Is this the man thou meanest!

MESSENGER
This is he.

OEDIPUS
And now old man, look up and answer all
I ask thee. Wast thou once of Laius'
    house?

HERDSMAN
I was, a thrall, not purchased but home-
bred.

OEDIPUS
What was thy business? how wast thou
employed?

HERDSMAN
The best part of my life I tended sheep.

OEDIPUS
What were the pastures thou didst most
frequent?

HERDSMAN
Cithaeron and the neighboring alps.

OEDIPUS
Then there
Thou must have known yon man, at least
by fame?

HERDSMAN
Yon man? in what way? what man dost
thou mean?

OEDIPUS
The man here, having met him in past
times...

HERDSMAN
Off-hand I cannot call him well to mind.

MESSENGER
No wonder, master. But I will revive
His blunted memories. Sure he can recall
What time together both we drove our
    flocks,
He two, I one, on the Cithaeron range,
For three long summers; I his mate from
    spring
Till rose Arcturus; then in winter time
I led mine home, he his to Laius' folds.
Did these things happen as I say, or no?

HERDSMAN
'Tis long ago, but all thou say'st is true.

MESSENGER
Well, thou mast then remember giving me
A child to rear as my own foster-son?

HERDSMAN
Why dost thou ask this question? What of
    that?

MESSENGER
Friend, he that stands before thee was that
    child.

HERDSMAN
A plague upon thee! Hold thy wanton
    tongue!

OEDIPUS
Softly, old man, rebuke him not; thy words
Are more deserving chastisement than his.

HERDSMAN
O best of masters, what is my offense?

OEDIPUS
Not answering what he asks about the
    child.

HERDSMAN
He speaks at random, babbles like a fool.

OEDIPUS
If thou lack'st grace to speak, I'll loose thy
    tongue.

HERDSMAN
For mercy's sake abuse not an old man.

OEDIPUS
Arrest the villain, seize and pinion him!

HERDSMAN
Alack, alack!

What have I done? what wouldst thou fur-
    ther learn?

OEDIPUS
Didst give this man the child of whom he
    asks?

HERDSMAN
I did; and would that I had died that day!

OEDIPUS
And die thou shalt unless thou tell the
    truth.

HERDSMAN
But, if I tell it, I am doubly lost.

OEDIPUS
The knave methinks will still prevaricate.

HERDSMAN
Nay, I confessed I gave it long ago.

OEDIPUS
Whence came it? was it thine, or given to
    thee?

HERDSMAN
I had it from another, 'twas not mine.

OEDIPUS
From whom of these our townsmen, and
    what house?

HERDSMAN
Forbear for God's sake, master, ask no
    more.

OEDIPUS
If I must question thee again, thou'rt lost.

HERDSMAN
Well then—it was a child of Laius' house.

OEDIPUS
Slave-born or one of Laius' own race?

HERDSMAN
Ah me!
I stand upon the perilous edge of speech.

OEDIPUS
And I of hearing, but I still must hear.

HERDSMAN
Know then the child was by repute
    his own,
But she within, thy consort best could tell.

OEDIPUS
What! she, she gave it thee?

HERDSMAN
'Tis so, my king.

OEDIPUS
With what intent?

HERDSMAN
To make away with it.

OEDIPUS
What, she its mother.

HERDSMAN
Fearing a dread weird.

OEDIPUS
What weird?

HERDSMAN
'Twas told that he should slay his sire.

OEDIPUS
What didst thou give it then to this
    old man?

HERDSMAN
Through pity, master, for the babe. I
    thought
He'd take it to the country whence he
    came;
But he preserved it for the worst of woes.

For if thou art in sooth what this man
    saith,
God pity thee! thou wast to misery born.

OEDIPUS
Ah me! ah me! all brought to pass, all true!
O light, may I behold thee nevermore!
I stand a wretch, in birth, in wedlock
    cursed,
A parricide, incestuously, triply cursed!
[Exit OEDIPUS]

CHORUS
(Str. 1)
Races of mortal man
Whose life is but a span,
I count ye but the shadow of a shade!
For he who most doth know
Of bliss, hath but the show;
A moment, and the visions pale and fade.
Thy fall, O Oedipus, thy piteous fall
Warns me none born of women blest to
    call.

(Ant. 1)
For he of marksmen best,
O Zeus, outshot the rest,
And won the prize supreme of wealth and
    power.
By him the vulture maid
Was quelled, her witchery laid;

He rose our savior and the land's strong
  tower.
We hailed thee king and from that day
  adored
Of mighty Thebes the universal lord.

(Str. 2)
O heavy hand of fate!
Who now more desolate,
Whose tale more sad than thine, whose lot
  more dire?
O Oedipus, discrowned head,
Thy cradle was thy marriage bed;
One harborage sufficed for son and sire.
How could the soil thy father eared so long
Endure to bear in silence such a wrong?

(Ant. 2)
All-seeing Time hath caught
Guilt, and to justice brought
The son and sire commingled in one bed.
O child of Laius' ill-starred race
Would I had ne'er beheld thy face;
I raise for thee a dirge as o'er the dead.
Yet, sooth to say, through thee I drew new
  breath,
And now through thee I feel a second
  death.
[Enter SECOND MESSENGER.]

SECOND MESSENGER

Most grave and reverend senators of
        Thebes,
What Deeds ye soon must hear, what
        sights behold
How will ye mourn, if, true-born patriots,
Ye reverence still the race of Labdacus!
Not Ister nor all Phasis' flood, I ween,
Could wash away the blood-stains from
        this house,
The ills it shrouds or soon will bring to
        light,
Ills wrought of malice, not unwittingly.
The worst to bear are self-inflicted
        wounds.

CHORUS

Grievous enough for all our tears and
        groans
Our past calamities; what canst thou add?

SECOND MESSENGER

My tale is quickly told and quickly heard.
Our sovereign lady queen Jocasta's dead.

CHORUS

Alas, poor queen! how came she by her
        death?

SECOND MESSENGER

By her own hand. And all the horror of it,

Not having seen, yet cannot comprehend.
Nathless, as far as my poor memory serves,
I will relate the unhappy lady's woe.
When in her frenzy she had passed inside
The vestibule, she hurried straight to win
The bridal-chamber, clutching at her hair
With both her hands, and, once within the
    room,
She shut the doors behind her with a
    crash.
"Laius," she cried, and called her husband
    dead
Long, long ago; her thought was of that
    child
By him begot, the son by whom the sire
Was murdered and the mother left to
    breed
With her own seed, a monstrous progeny.
Then she bewailed the marriage bed
    whereon
Poor wretch, she had conceived a double
    brood,
Husband by husband, children by her
    child.
What happened after that I cannot tell,
Nor how the end befell, for with a shriek
Burst on us Oedipus; all eyes were fixed
On Oedipus, as up and down he strode,
Nor could we mark her agony to the end.
For stalking to and fro "A sword!" he
    cried,

"Where is the wife, no wife, the teeming
      womb
That bore a double harvest, me and
      mine?"
And in his frenzy some supernal power
(No mortal, surely, none of us who
      watched him)
Guided his footsteps; with a terrible shriek,
As though one beckoned him, he crashed
      against
The folding doors, and from their staples
      forced
The wrenched bolts and hurled himself
      within.
Then we beheld the woman hanging
      there,
A running noose entwined about her neck.
But when he saw her, with a maddened
      roar
He loosed the cord; and when her
      wretched corpse
Lay stretched on earth, what followed—O
      'twas dread!
He tore the golden brooches that upheld
Her queenly robes, upraised them high
      and smote
Full on his eye-balls, uttering words like
      these:
"No more shall ye behold such sights
      of woe,

Deeds I have suffered and myself have
    wrought;
Henceforward quenched in darkness shall
    ye see
Those ye should ne'er have seen; now
    blind to those
Whom, when I saw, I vainly yearned to
    know."
Such was the burden of his moan,
    whereto,
Not once but oft, he struck with his hand
    uplift
His eyes, and at each stroke the ensan-
    guined orbs
Bedewed his beard, not oozing drop by
    drop,
But one black gory downpour, thick as
    hail.
Such evils, issuing from the double source,
Have whelmed them both, confounding
    man and wife.
Till now the storied fortune of this house
Was fortunate indeed; but from this day
Woe, lamentation, ruin, death, disgrace,
All ills that can be named, all, all are
    theirs.

CHORUS
But hath he still no respite from his pain?

SECOND MESSENGER

He cries, "Unbar the doors and let all
    Thebes
Behold the slayer of his sire, his
    mother's—"
That shameful word my lips may not
    repeat.
He vows to fly self-banished from the land,
Nor stay to bring upon his house the curse
Himself had uttered; but he has no
    strength
Nor one to guide him, and his torture's
    more
Than man can suffer, as yourselves
    will see.
For lo, the palace portals are unbarred,
And soon ye shall behold a sight so sad
That he who must abhorred would pity it.
[Enter OEDIPUS blinded.]

CHORUS

Woeful sight! more woeful none
These sad eyes have looked upon.
Whence this madness? None can tell
Who did cast on thee his spell,
    prowling all thy life around,
Leaping with a demon bound.
Hapless wretch! how can I brook
On thy misery to look?
Though to gaze on thee I yearn,
Much to question, much to learn,

Horror-struck away I turn.

OEDIPUS
Ah me! ah woe is me!
Ah whither am I borne!
How like a ghost forlorn
My voice flits from me on the air!
On, on the demon goads. The end, ah
    where?

CHORUS
An end too dread to tell, too dark to see.

OEDIPUS
(Str. 1)
Dark, dark! The horror of darkness, like a
    shroud,
Wraps me and bears me on through mist
    and cloud.
Ah me, ah me! What spasms athwart me
    shoot,
What pangs of agonizing memory?

CHORUS
No marvel if in such a plight thou feel'st
The double weight of past and present
    woes.

OEDIPUS
(Ant. 1)
Ah friend, still loyal, constant still and
    kind,
Thou carest for the blind.
I know thee near, and though bereft of
    eyes,
Thy voice I recognize.

CHORUS
O doer of dread deeds, how couldst
    thou mar
Thy vision thus? What demon goaded
    thee?

OEDIPUS
(Str. 2)
Apollo, friend, Apollo, he it was
That brought these ills to pass;
But the right hand that dealt the blow
Was mine, none other. How,
How, could I longer see when sight
Brought no delight?

CHORUS
Alas! 'tis as thou sayest.

OEDIPUS
Say, friends, can any look or voice
Or touch of love henceforth my heart
    rejoice?

Haste, friends, no fond delay,
Take the twice cursed away
Far from all ken,
The man abhorred of gods, accursed
    of men.

CHORUS
O thy despair well suits thy desperate case.
Would I had never looked upon thy face!

OEDIPUS
(Ant. 2)
My curse on him whoe'er unrived
The waif's fell fetters and my life revived!
He meant me well, yet had he left me
    there,
He had saved my friends and me a world
    of care.

CHORUS
I too had wished it so.

OEDIPUS
Then had I never come to shed
My father's blood nor climbed my moth-
    er's bed;
The monstrous offspring of a womb
    defiled,
Co-mate of him who gendered me, and
    child.
Was ever man before afflicted thus,

Like Oedipus.

CHORUS
I cannot say that thou hast counseled well,
For thou wert better dead than living
    blind.

OEDIPUS
What's done was well done. Thou canst
    never shake
My firm belief. A truce to argument.
For, had I sight, I know not with what eyes
I could have met my father in the shades,
Or my poor mother, since against the
    twain
I sinned, a sin no gallows could atone.
Aye, but, ye say, the sight of children joys
A parent's eyes. What, born as mine were
    born?
No, such a sight could never bring me joy;
Nor this fair city with its battlements,
Its temples and the statues of its gods,
Sights from which I, now wretchedst of all,
Once ranked the foremost Theban in all
    Thebes,
By my own sentence am cut off,
    condemned
By my own proclamation 'gainst the
    wretch,
The miscreant by heaven itself declared
Unclean—and of the race of Laius.

Thus branded as a felon by myself,
How had I dared to look you in the face?
Nay, had I known a way to choke the
    springs
Of hearing, I had never shrunk to make
A dungeon of this miserable frame,
Cut off from sight and hearing; for 'tis
    bliss
to bide in regions sorrow cannot reach.
Why didst thou harbor me, Cithaeron,
    why
Didst thou not take and slay me? Then I
    never
Had shown to men the secret of my birth.
O Polybus, O Corinth, O my home,
Home of my ancestors (so wast thou
    called)
How fair a nursling then I seemed,
    how foul
The canker that lay festering in the bud!
Now is the blight revealed of root and
    fruit.
Ye triple high-roads, and thou hidden
    glen,
Coppice, and pass where meet the three-
    branched ways,
Ye drank my blood, the life-blood these
    hands spilt,
My father's; do ye call to mind perchance
Those deeds of mine ye witnessed and
    the work

I wrought thereafter when I came to
    Thebes?
O fatal wedlock, thou didst give me birth,
And, having borne me, sowed again my
    seed,
Mingling the blood of fathers, brothers,
    children,
Brides, wives and mothers, an incestuous
    brood,
All horrors that are wrought beneath
    the sun,
Horrors so foul to name them were
    unmeet.
O, I adjure you, hide me anywhere
Far from this land, or slay me straight, or
    cast me
Down to the depths of ocean out of sight.
Come hither, deign to touch an abject
    wretch;
Draw near and fear not; I myself
    must bear
The load of guilt that none but I can
    share.
[Enter CREON.]

CREON
Lo, here is Creon, the one man to grant
Thy prayer by action or advice, for he
Is left the State's sole guardian in thy stead.

OEDIPUS
Ah me! what words to accost him can I
    find?
What cause has he to trust me? In the past
I have bee proved his rancorous enemy.

CREON
Not in derision, Oedipus, I come
Nor to upbraid thee with thy past
    misdeeds.
(To BYSTANDERS)
But shame upon you! if ye feel no sense
Of human decencies, at least revere
The Sun whose light beholds and nurtures
    all.
Leave not thus nakedly for all to gaze at
A horror neither earth nor rain from
    heaven
Nor light will suffer. Lead him straight
    within,
For it is seemly that a kinsman's woes
Be heard by kin and seen by kin alone.

OEDIPUS
O listen, since thy presence comes to me
A shock of glad surprise—so noble thou,
And I so vile—O grant me one small
    boon.
I ask it not on my behalf, but thine.

CREON
And what the favor thou wouldst crave
    of me?

OEDIPUS
Forth from thy borders thrust me with all
    speed;
Set me within some vasty desert where
No mortal voice shall greet me any more.

CREON
This had I done already, but I deemed
It first behooved me to consult the god.

OEDIPUS
His will was set forth fully—to destroy
The parricide, the scoundrel; and I am he.

CREON
Yea, so he spake, but in our present plight
'Twere better to consult the god anew.

OEDIPUS
Dare ye inquire concerning such a wretch?

CREON
Yea, for thyself wouldst credit now his
    word.

OEDIPUS
Aye, and on thee in all humility

I lay this charge: let her who lies within
Receive such burial as thou shalt ordain;
Such rites 'tis thine, as brother, to perform.
But for myself, O never let my Thebes,
The city of my sires, be doomed to bear
The burden of my presence while I live.
No, let me be a dweller on the hills,
On yonder mount Cithaeron, famed as
    mine,
My tomb predestined for me by my sire
And mother, while they lived, that I
    may die
Slain as they sought to slay me, when alive.
This much I know full surely, nor disease
Shall end my days, nor any common
    chance;
For I had ne'er been snatched from death,
    unless
I was predestined to some awful doom.
So be it. I reck not how Fate deals with me
But my unhappy children—for my sons
Be not concerned, O Creon, they
    are men,
And for themselves, where'er they be, can
    fend.
But for my daughters twain, poor innocent
    maids,
Who ever sat beside me at the board
Sharing my viands, drinking of my cup,
For them, I pray thee, care, and, if thou
    willst,

O might I feel their touch and make my
    moan.
Hear me, O prince, my noble-hearted
    prince!
Could I but blindly touch them with my
    hands
I'd think they still were mine, as when
    I saw.
[ANTIGONE and ISMENE are led in.]
What say I? can it be my pretty ones
Whose sobs I hear? Has Creon pitied me
And sent me my two darlings? Can
    this be?

CREON

'Tis true; 'twas I procured thee this
    delight,
Knowing the joy they were to thee of old.

OEDIPUS

God speed thee! and as meed for bringing
    them
May Providence deal with thee kindlier
Than it has dealt with me! O children
    mine,
Where are ye? Let me clasp you with these
    hands,
A brother's hands, a father's; hands
    that made
Lack-luster sockets of his once bright eyes;
Hands of a man who blindly, recklessly,

Became your sire by her from whom he
    sprang.
Though I cannot behold you, I must weep
In thinking of the evil days to come,
The slights and wrongs that men will put
    upon you.
Where'er ye go to feast or festival,
No merrymaking will it prove for you,
But oft abashed in tears ye will return.
And when ye come to marriageable years,
Where's the bold wooers who will
    jeopardize
To take unto himself such disrepute
As to my children's children still must
    cling,
For what of infamy is lacking here?
"Their father slew his father, sowed
    the seed
Where he himself was gendered, and
    begat
These maidens at the source wherefrom he
    sprang."
Such are the gibes that men will cast
    at you.
Who then will wed you? None, I ween,
    but ye
Must pine, poor maids, in single bar-
    renness.
O Prince, Menoeceus' son, to thee, I turn,
With the it rests to father them, for we
Their natural parents, both of us, are lost.

O leave them not to wander poor, unwed,
Thy kin, nor let them share my low estate.
O pity them so young, and but for thee
All destitute. Thy hand upon it, Prince.
To you, my children I had much to say,
Were ye but ripe to hear. Let this suffice:
Pray ye may find some home and live
    content,
And may your lot prove happier than your
    sire's.

CREON
Thou hast had enough of weeping; pass
    within.

OEDIPUS
I must obey,
Though 'tis grievous.

CREON
Weep not, everything must have its day.

OEDIPUS
Well I go, but on conditions.

CREON
What thy terms for going, say.

OEDIPUS
Send me from the land an exile.

CREON
Ask this of the gods, not me.

OEDIPUS
But I am the gods' abhorrence.

CREON
Then they soon will grant thy plea.

OEDIPUS
Lead me hence, then, I am willing.

CREON
Come, but let thy children go.

OEDIPUS
Rob me not of these my children!

CREON
Crave not mastery in all,
For the mastery that raised thee was thy
      bane and wrought thy fall.

CHORUS
Look ye, countrymen and Thebans, this is
      Oedipus the great,
He who knew the Sphinx's riddle and was
      mightiest in our state.
Who of all our townsmen gazed not on his
      fame with envious eyes?

Now, in what a sea of troubles sunk and
   overwhelmed he lies!
Therefore wait to see life's ending ere thou
   count one mortal blest;
Wait till free from pain and sorrow he has
   gained his final rest.

---

1. Dr. Kennedy and others render "Since to men of experience I see that also comparisons of their counsels are in
   most lively use."
2. Literally "not to call them thine," but the Greek may be
   rendered "In order not to reveal thine."
3. The Greek text that occurs in this place has been lost.

Made in United States
North Haven, CT
25 July 2023

39465184R00064